DAD JOKES

The
Cheesy
Edition

An Hachette UK Company

www.hachette.co.uk

First published in Great Britain in 2020 by Cassell, an imprint of
Octopus Publishing Group Ltd
Carmelite House
50 Victoria Embankment
London EC4Y 0DZ
www.octopusbooks.co.uk

Distributed in the US by
Hachette Book Group
1290 Avenue of the Americas
4th and 5th Floors
New York, NY 10104

Distributed in Canada by
Canadian Manda Group
664 Annette St.
Toronto, Ontario, Canada M6S 2C8

ISBN 978 1 78840 246 0

A CIP catalogue record for this book is available from the
British Library. Printed in China.

10 9 8 7 6 5 4

Publishing Director: Stephanie Jackson
Editorial Assistant: George Brooker
Designer: The Oak Studio
Senior Designer: Jaz Bahra
Production Controller: Serena Savini

DAD JOKES

The Cheesy Edition

– From the Instagram sensation –
@DadSaysJokes

CASSELL
ILLUSTRATED

Dedicated to Major Peter Chilvers,
a thoroughly decent fellow with
a very dry wit.

Introduction

Not another dad jokes book I hear you say?
Well... yes! As long as there are people, there
will be laughter. And here at @DadSaysJokes
we like to keep the laughter coming – so catch
up with the ultimate cheesy humour in our
third volume.

Thanks again to our very vocal and ever
growing community on Instagram, Twitter and
Facebook. Your timely ripostes and razor-sharp
wit breathe new life into the oldest, cheesiest
chestnuts.

Let's all continue to make the world a happier
place – and please keep those jolly japes
coming. We really couldn't have done this
without you.

Lots of love and laughter,

Kit & Andrew

My neighbour tiled my roof for free.

He said it was on the house.

_____

A guy walks into a psychiatrist's office wearing see-through shorts.

The psychiatrist says: "Well, I can clearly see your nuts."

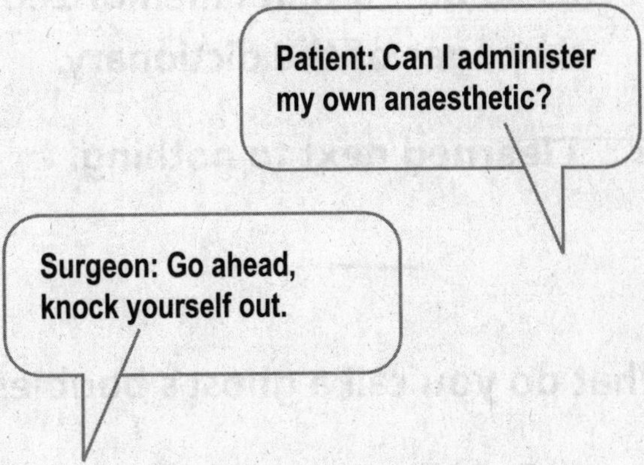
Patient: Can I administer my own anaesthetic?
Surgeon: Go ahead, knock yourself out.

I was so bored that I memorized
six pages of the dictionary.

I learned next to nothing.

What do you call a ghost's boobies?

Paranormal en-titties.

I just started a business where we specialize in weighing tiny objects.

It's a small-scale operation.

What do you call a failed gathering of crows?

An attempted murder.

_____

I took my eight-year-old girl to the office with me on Bring Your Child to Work Day. As we walked around the office, she starting crying, so I asked her what was wrong.

As my colleagues gathered round, she sobbed: "But Daddy, where are all the clowns you said you worked with?"

You know what happens if you don't pay your exorcist?

You get repossessed.

I made some fish tacos last night.

But they just ignored them and swam away.

Did you hear about the mathematician who's afraid of negative numbers?

He'll stop at nothing to avoid them.

———

How do you cut an ocean in two?

With a sea-saw.

Seven has "even" in it.

That's odd.

_____

I was in the supermarket the other day when this guy threw a block of Cheddar at me.

Outraged, I shouted: "Well, that's not very mature, is it?!"

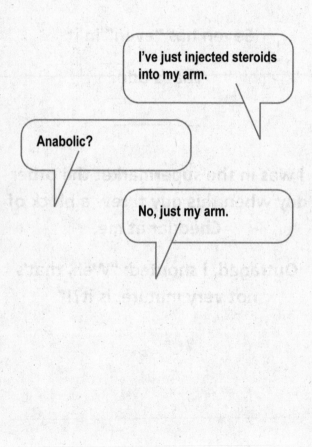

My wife said she'd leave me if I didn't stop eating pasta.

Now I'm feeling cannelloni.

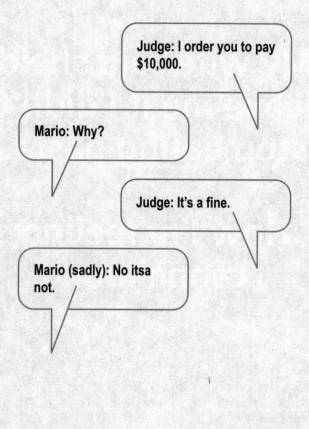

What's the worst thing about being an egg?

You only get laid once.

_____

We all know that 6 was scared of 7 because 7, 8, 9. But *why* did 7 eat 9?

Because you're supposed to eat three squared meals a day.

My addiction
to Viagra . . .

. . . was the hardest
time of my life.

What's the most effective way to quit being vegan?

Cold turkey.

———

What should you do if you're addicted to seaweed?

Sea kelp.

If the earth was flat and fish swam over the edge, where would they go?

Trout-er space.

Common sense is like deodorant.

Those who need it never use it.

I just quit my job at the helium factory.

I won't be spoken to in that tone.

_____

I was driving home the other day
when suddenly a group of robbers
jumped in and stole everything.

They were pirates of the car I be in.

Did you hear about the man who fell into the upholstery machine?

He's fully recovered.

———

My dad told me he always struggled with three subjects in school.

One was maths, and he couldn't remember the other one.

What do you call a snail in a boat?

A snailor.

The World Health Organization has declared that dogs cannot transmit coronavirus, so there is no reason to quarantine dogs anymore.

W.H.O. let the dogs out!

I was in New Mexico and a cowboy asked me if I could help round up 18 cows.

"Yes, of course," I said. "That would be 20 cows."

_____

What did one plate say to the other?

"Lunch is on me!"

I trapped a couple of vegan burglars in my basement. At least I think they were vegan.

They kept shouting: "Lettuce leaf!"

FUN FACT:

If you sneeze and fart at the same time . . .

. . . your body takes a screenshot.

When I was in college, I used to live on a houseboat. I started dating the girl next door.

Eventually, we drifted apart.

_____

I've got some racing geese for sale.

Let me know if you want a quick gander.

I bought a knife that can cut through four loaves of bread at once.

It's a four-loaf cleaver.

Did you hear about the chameleon
that couldn't change colour?

He had a reptile dysfunction.

———

What did the tectonic plate say when it
bumped into another tectonic plate?

"Sorry, that's my fault."

My friend told me he put a potato down his swimming trunks and now the girls won't leave him alone.

It didn't work for me. Apparently, you're meant to put it down the front.

———————

What is it called when two mummies fart at the same time?

Toot-in-common.

I just went into Starbucks and the barista was wearing a face mask . . .

Me: "Why are you wearing a surgical mask?"

Barista: "I'm not; it's a coughy filter."

Due to the quarantine . . .

. . . I'll only be telling inside jokes.

I'd been a bee-keeper for years, but then my crush said: "It's me or those nasty insects – make up your mind."

At first, I didn't think she was serious.

Then I saw her face.

Now I'm a bee-leaver.

Why don't vampires bet on horses?

They can't handle the stakes.

I recently switched all the labels
on my wife's spice rack.

She hasn't noticed yet, but the
thyme is cumin.

I just bought the perfect tool for making a good Indian flatbread.

It's a naan-stick pan.

Stephen King has a son named Joe.

I'm not joking, but he is.

I made the mistake of telling my suitcases that we won't be going anywhere this year because of the pandemic.

I'm having to put up with a lot of emotional baggage.

———————

What do you call a slow bullet?
A slug.

I opened a shop selling used artificial limbs.

I called it the second-hand second hand store.

———————————

It's OK if you have no idea what "prefix" means.

It's not the end of the word.

I was driving on the highway with my wife, and she said: "Hey, you missed a right!"

"Thanks, babe," I said. "You MRS Right."

If you're ever attacked by a mob of clowns . . .

. . . go for the juggler.

A sperm donor, a carpenter and Julius Caesar walked into a bar.

He came, he saw, he conquered.

My wife was disappointed to find out why my nickname in college was "The Love Machine".

It was because I sucked at tennis.

———————

What do you call a superhero with a bad sense of direction?

Wander Woman.

If I have twin daughters,
I'll name one Kate . . .

. . . and I'll name the other Dupli-Kate.

———

I think my phone is broken.

I pressed the "home" button,
but I'm still at work.

My great-uncle died while making butter on his farm last week.

It was a really unfortunate churn of events.

———————

My friends and I are in a band called Bedsheets.

We're a covers band.

For the past three weeks, I've been jogging a mile a day.

Now I don't know where I am.

What do you call a bunch of crows inside a tent?

Murder within tent.

_____

Did you know that 97 per cent of the world is stupid?

Luckily, I'm in the other 5 per cent.

What lies on the ground,
100 feet in the air?

A dead centipede.

_____

If I don't perfect human cloning . . .

I won't be able to live with myself.

I ran out of toilet paper and am now reduced to wiping with lettuce leaves.

Today was the tip of the iceberg. Tomorrow? That romaines to be seen.

A small meteorite is reportedly headed for Legoland.

The damage is expected to be 50 square blocks.

William Shatner wanted to start up
a line of women's underwear.

Unfortunately, Shatner Panties wasn't
the greatest brand name.

———————

I always carry a picture of my wife
and children in my wallet.

It reminds me why there's
no money in there.

What's the world's saddest
kind of pizza?

Pepper-lonely.

———————

I invented a new word today.

Plagiarism.

I got my best friend a fridge for his birthday.

I can't wait to see his face light up when he opens it.

What did Delaware?

Maybe a New Jersey? I don't know, but Alaska.

My father doesn't trust anyone. In fact, he has a saying . . .

But he won't tell me what it is.

Doctor: Your brain fell out after your accident, but we managed to put it back in.

Patient: Thanks for reminding me.

I can't find my *Gone in 60 Seconds* DVD.

It was here a minute ago.

———

My son asked me what
procrastinate means.

I said: "I'll tell you later."

What do you call a bee that never quite made it?

A wanna bee.

_____

Why did the "A" go to the bathroom and come out as an "E"?

It had a vowel movement.

What's the difference between an actor and a burned rodent?

One's Chris Pratt, the other is a crisp rat.

_____

Hi, I'm Buzz Aldrin, the second person to step on the Moon.

Neil before me.

What was Icarus's favourite food?

Hot wings.

"Sorry sir, we don't serve time travellers here."

A time traveller walks into a bar.

———————

Don't you just hate it when you're picking up your bags at the airport, and everyone's luggage is better than yours?

Worst-case scenario.

Restaurant manager: Why do you think you would make a good waiter?

Me: I bring a lot to the table.

If anyone gets a message from me about canned meat, don't open it!

It's spam.

———

Today is my 42nd birthday. I just announced to my kids that, finally . . .

. . . I have fortitude.

Yesterday, I was washing the car with my son.

He said: "Dad, can't you just use a sponge?"

I just finished reading a book about the greatest basement that ever existed.

It was a best cellar.

What do you call people who hate long sentences?

Criminals.

You know what's really odd?

Numbers not divisible by 2.

_____

My wife is threatening to leave me because of my obsession with acting like a news anchor.

More on this after the break.

What do clouds wear under their shorts?

Thunderpants.

_____

I just won an award for most secretive person in the office.

I can't tell you how much that means to me.

I'm organizing a charity ball next week for people who struggle to reach orgasm.

Just let me know if you can't come.

_____

When Dad died, he left me his Subaru.

It was his final legacy.

My wife gave me an ultimatum. It was either her or my addiction to sweets.

The decision was a piece of cake.

I went to the pharmacy yesterday and asked the assistant what gets rid of the coronavirus.

She said: "Ammonia cleaner."

"Sorry," I said. "I thought you worked here."

It's really hard to say what my wife does for a living.

She sells seashells on the seashore.

British people be like: "I'm Bri'ish."

I guess they drank the "t".

I once dreamed that I was a muffler.

I woke up exhausted.

———

According to ancient Japanese lore,
the colour of a person's aura changes
right before they die.

Cyan-aura.

Last night when I was drunk, I tried to impress a girl by swallowing a bunch of Scrabble tiles.

My next trip to the bathroom could spell disaster.

_____

I asked a gardener which herbs were snitches.

He said only thyme would tell.

My wife tripped and fell while carrying a pile of clothes she had just finished ironing.

I watched it all unfold.

If you boil a funny bone . . .

. . . you get a laughing stock.

My friend is getting rich by taking pictures of salmon dressed in human clothes.

It's like shooting fish in apparel.

Harry has decided to go into acting with his wife, Meghan Markle.

His stage name will be the Artist Formerly Known as Prince.

A shop assistant tried to stop an armed robber by attacking him with a labelling gun.

Police are now looking for a man with a price on his head.

Why would a pig dressed in black never get bullied?

Because Batman has sworn to protect goth ham.

———————

My first time using an elevator was an uplifting experience, but the second time brought me down.

My wife accused me of trying to win every argument we had . . .

. . . so I told her why that was wrong.

———————

What do you call a sword that doesn't weigh much?

A light saber.

More than a century ago, two brothers claimed that it was possible to fly.

They were Wright.

Is it crazy how saying sentences backwards . . .

. . . creates backwards sentences saying how crazy it is?

I got bored watching the earth turn, so, after 24 hours, I called it a day.

———————

What did the hat say to the scarf?

"I'll hang around here. You go on ahead."

My friend says he's a compulsive liar . . .

I don't believe him.

———

A man walked into a bar.

Lucky bastard.

During my career as a lumberjack, I cut down exactly 52,487 trees.

I know because I kept a log.

I scared the mailman today by coming to the door naked.

I don't know what scared him most: the fact that I was naked, or the fact that I knew where he lived.

———————

To the person who stole my glasses:

I can still drink from the bottle.

Does Sean Connery like herbs?

Yes, but only partially.

———————

The person who invented autocorrect should burn in hello.

What do you give a dog that has a high temperature?

Mustard – it's the best thing for a hot dog.

_____

I was watching a documentary about a woman who got breast implants made of wood.

I thought to myself: "That would hurt, wooden tit?"

My doctor wrote
me a prescription
for daily sex . . .

But my wife insists
it says dyslexia.

I went to a cannibal wedding.
The groom toasted the bridesmaids,
the best man toasted the bride and
groom, and the father of the bride
toasted absent friends . . .

It was one hell of a barbecue.

———

The pub was pretty wild last night.

Someone's nipple got pierced – and
I got banned from darts.

On Monday, we start Diarrhoea Awareness Week.

Runs until Friday.

———

What kind of fish work in hospitals?

Sturgeons.

My right arm hurts like crazy, but only between nine and eleven a.m.

Worst case of ten-ish elbow ever.

———

What did Kim Jong-un say
before he died?

My Korea is over.

A week before Grandad died,
we bought him a snowboard.

He went downhill very quickly
after that.

_____

I complimented my imaginary friend
the other day.

He was made up.

My mother always used to say: "The way to a man's heart is through his stomach."

Lovely woman; terrible surgeon.

What do you call a lawyer when he's cooking dinner?

A sue chef.

I hear in Africa they tried an experiment where they blessed the rains.

It was a Toto failure.

The other day I saw a bucket at the hardware store with a sign that said: "Dead batteries – half price".

I thought to myself: "These should be free of charge."

I once bought a wooden car: wooden engine, wooden doors, wooden wheels, wooden seats. I put the wooden key in the wooden ignition.

Wooden start.

This morning, my son said his ear hurt. I asked: "On the inside or on the outside?"

So, he walked out the front door, then came back in and said: "Both."

I do really feel bad for the Class of 2020. People say your senior year flies.

I just didn't realize it would Zoom.

My friend claims that he "accidentally" glued himself to his autobiography. I don't believe him . . .

. . . but that's his story, and he's sticking to it.

My wife is so negative. I remembered the car seat, the stroller AND the diaper bag.

Yet all she can talk about is how I forgot the baby.

Why was the baby jalapeño shivering?

He was a little chilli.

**What did the mermaid wear
to maths class?**

An algae-bra.

_____

A German tourist jumped into a freezing
river to save my dog. After he climbed
out, he said: "Here is ze dog. Dry him off
and keep him warm, he vill be fine."

I asked him, "Are you a vet?"

"Vet?" he said. "I'm bloody soaking."

What's the difference between a constipated owl and a bad marksman?

A bad marksman shoots but can't hit; a constipated owl hoots but can't shit.

My friend Jack claims he can communicate with vegetables.

Jack and the beans talk.

My friend went completely bald years ago, but he still carries a comb with him.

He just can't part with it.

Did you hear about the guy getting hit by the same bicycle every single day, day after day?

It was a vicious cycle.

_____

I took my car to the mechanic because it was making a terrible noise.

He removed the Mariah Carey Christmas CD and now it's fine.

I was sacked from the ice-cream factory today.

It was because I'll only work on two sundaes a month.

My girlfriend threatened to leave me if I didn't stop pointing out random exits and entrances.

I said: "There's the door."

Boss: You are the worst train operator ever. How many trains have you derailed in the past year?

Me: I'm not sure. It's hard to keep track.

Most people like to have the time off between Christmas and New Year, but I have a better idea.

I'd like to have the time off between New Year and Christmas.

Why did the large bucket think the small bucket was sick?

It was a little pail.

My wife told me: "Sex is better on holiday."

I wasn't expecting to read that on the postcard she sent to me from Greece.

Did you hear about McDonald's trying to get into the steakhouse market?

It was a big McSteak.

Just learned
the word for
constipation
in German.

Farfrompoopen.

Son: What rhymes with purple?

Dad: No, it doesn't!

Why was 2019 afraid of 2020?

Because they got into a fight and 2021.

_____

My wife dressed up as a police officer and told me I was under arrest on suspicion of being good in bed.

After two minutes, all charges were dropped due to a lack of evidence.

A sheep, a drum and a snake fall
off a cliff . . .

Baa-dumm-tsss.

What type of cake makes you
stop having sex?

Wedding cake.

I just read a book about the history of glue.

Couldn't put it down.

———

My wife tried to take a selfie in the sauna but it was too blurry.

She has selfie steam issues.

Two goldfish are in a tank.

One says to the other: "Do you know how to drive this thing?"

———————

Today a man knocked on my door and asked for a small donation towards the local swimming pool.

I gave him a glass of water.

The last thing my grandfather said before he died was: "It's always worth investing in good-quality speakers."

That was some sound advice.

Ladies, if he can't appreciate your jokes about fruit . . .

. . . you need to let that mango!

———

Scientists definitively confirmed today that anteaters are incapable of contracting coronavirus.

Apparently, they're filled with anty-bodies.

I went into a pet shop and asked for 12 bees. The shopkeeper counted out 13 and handed them over.

"You've given me one too many," I said.

"The extra one is a freebie."

———————

What's a cannibal's favourite game?

Swallow the leader.

A golfer and a
caddy step on to
the golf course . . .

Caddy: "Sir, why
did you bring
two bags?"

Golfer: "In case I get
a hole in one."

Why do North Koreans draw the straightest lines?

Because they have a supreme ruler.

What did the cannibal's wife say when he came home late for dinner?

"I'm giving you the cold shoulder."

My wife is like a newspaper.

There's a new issue every day.

———

Did you know vampires aren't real?

Unless you Count Dracula.

Why did the sad ghost use an elevator?

To lift his spirits.

**What's the difference between
a coyote and a flea?**

**One howls on the prairie while the
other prowls on the hairy.**

What do you call an annoyed lobster?

A frustacean.

I was feeling lonely so I bought some shares.

It's nice to have some company.

I walked into a bank, pointed a long, thin piece of wood at the ceiling and shouted: "This is a stick up!"

Where do lizards go to fix their fallen tails?

The retail shop.

To ride a horse or not to ride a horse.

That is equestrian.

Dentists always ask dumb questions, like: "When was the last time you flossed?"

Bro – you were there!

———————

I asked my wife for an audiobook this Christmas, but she got me an encyclopaedia instead.

That speaks volumes.

How did Mary and Joseph know that Jesus was 8lb 2oz when he was born?

They had a weigh in a manger.

A guy died from laughing too much.

It was manslaughter.

What do pigs learn in the army?

Ham to ham combat.

The other day, my friend told me
I was delusional.

I nearly fell off my unicorn.

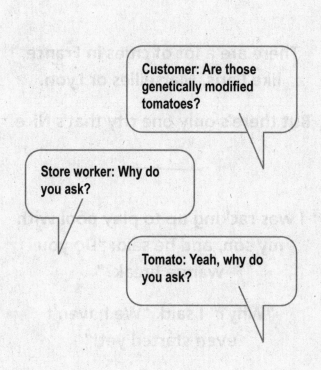

There are a lot of cities in France, like Paris, Marseilles or Lyon.

But there's only one city that's Nice.

————————

I was racking up to play pool with my son, and he said: "Do you wanna break?"

"Why?" I said. "We haven't even started yet!"

I found out my girlfriend is really a ghost.

I had my suspicions the moment she walked through the door.

Did you hear about the guy who invented the door knocker?

He won the no-bell prize.

_____

How do dancers ensure job stability during the COVID-19 crisis?

They twerk from home.

What do you call a zombie who cooks stir-fries?

Dead man wok-ing.

Don't be worried about your smartphone or TV spying on you. Your vacuum cleaner has been gathering dirt on you for years.

There's a new restaurant named Karma.

It doesn't have a menu. You just get what you deserve.

I spent $80 on a belt that didn't fit.

My wife said it was a huge waist.

I was at the museum and saw a painting of a bowl, with milk and some kind of food inside.

It was surreal.

———————

Do you remember when people started buying up all the toilet paper?

They were really losing their shit.

What do you call a zombified piece of toast?

The un-bread.

Believing in 12.5 per cent of the Bible makes you an eighth-theist.

When I die, I want to die peacefully, in my sleep, just like my granddad.

Not screaming hysterically like his passengers.

———

Farting in a packed elevator . . .

It's wrong on so many levels.

I want to dedicate this dad joke
to my father, who is a roofer.

So, Dad, if you're up there . . .

How do Vikings send secret messages?

Norse code.

I have a pen
that can write
underwater.

It can also write
other words, too.

What happens to an egg every time you look at it?

It becomes egg-sighted.

———————

Today was my first day as a waiter.

Me: "Sir, how would you like your steak?"

Customer: "Well done."

Me: "Thanks, that means a lot. I was terribly nervous earlier."

Our friend Chuck hasn't contacted us for months, so we renamed him Huck.

Because long time, no C.

A man is buying one banana, one apple and two eggs.

The cashier says: "You must be single."

The man answers: "Wow, how did you know that?"

The cashier says: "Because you're ugly."

Student: Are "well" and "actually" both single-syllable words?

Teacher: Well, yes, but actually, no.

How do locomotives hear?

Through the engineers.

———

What do snails become when they die?

Escarghosts.

What do you call a participation trophy in astronomy?

A constellation prize.

———

Before my surgery, the anaesthetist gave me a choice: she could knock me out with gas or a boat paddle.

It was an ether/oar situation.

My wife said she's leaving me because of I'm obsessed with tennis, and I'm too old.

I said: "I'm only 40, love."

———————

Why was the broom late for the meeting?

It overswept.

A man was recently hospitalized with six plastic horses up his butt. Doctors have described his condition as stable.

I'm allergic to bread, but I eat it anyway.

I'm a gluten for punishment.

_____

What do you call a crocodile that
is a detective?

An investi-gator.

Over the weekend I took my wife
to the theatre to see a performance
that was all about puns.

It was a play on words.

_____

I changed my iPod's name to Titanic.

It's syncing now.

My friend Barry drew a picture of me.
But that's OK, because . . .

. . . I Drew Barrymore.

My girlfriend wants me to choose
between her and my career as
a reporter.

I have some breaking news for her.

If a group of dolphins is called a pod and a group of crows is called a murder, what is a group of small children called?

Annoying.

———

I asked my wife to rate my listening skills. She said: "You're an 8 on a scale of 10."

I still don't get why she wanted me to urinate on a skeleton.

I was in a restaurant, and I said to the waitress: "Excuse me, can I ask you something about the menu please?"

To my surprise, the waitress slapped me across the face and said: "The men I please are none of your business!"

———

My wife wanted to brighten up the garden, so I planted some bulbs.

I tried to make a
pandemic joke
a while back.

Nobody laughed
at the time,
but eventually
everyone got it.

What do you call a bacterial disease caused by a pair of grizzlies?

Two-bear-culosis.

I was struggling to get my wife's attention, so I simply sat down and looked comfortable.

That did the trick.

A truck loaded with Vicks VapoRub
overturned on the highway.

Amazingly, there was no congestion
for eight hours.

A thief broke into my house last night
looking for money.

I got out of bed to look with him.

**What starts with T, ends with T
and is full of T?**

Teapot.

———————

I just heard that Kim Jong-un is sick.

I guess that makes him Kim Jong-ill.

I warned my daughter about using her whistle inside the house today and gave her one last chance . . .

Unfortunately, she blew it.

———————

My next-door neighbour and I were good friends, so we decided to share our water supply.

We got a long well.

What kind of doctor was Dr Pepper?

A fizz-ician.

To the two criminals who stole my calendar: I hope you both get six months.

———————

Nail salons closed, hair salons closed, tanning salons closed, waxing salons closed . . .

It's about to get ugly out there.

I'm making a new documentary
on how to fly a plane.

We're currently filming the pilot.

———————

My friend says I'm getting fat,
but in my defence . . .

. . . I've had a lot on my plate recently.

A neutron walks into a bar...

Neutron: "How much for a beer?"

Bartender: "For you? No charge."

**What is a scientist's favourite
kind of dog?**

Labs.

**My nickname at work is
Mr Compromise.**

**It wasn't my first choice,
but I'm OK with it.**

A lumberjack went into a magic forest. When he got there, he started to swing his axe to cut down a tree. The tree shouted: "Wait! I'm a talking tree!"

The lumberjack grinned. "And you will dialogue."

———————

We all know where the Big Apple is, but does anyone know where the . . .

. . . Minneapolis?

I just found out that my new electric toothbrush is not waterproof.

I was shocked.

I couldn't follow the storyline of Stephen King's *It*.

There were too many Maine characters.

———————

Sadly, I've lost 20 per cent of my sight.

Sigh.

I know a guy who keeps stealing iPhones.

At some point, he's going to face time.

———————

I was on the phone with my wife and said: "I'm almost home, honey. Please put the coffee maker on."

After a 20-second pause, I asked: "You still there, sweetheart?"

"Yes," she said. "But I don't think the coffee maker wants to talk right now."

My Tinder bio says that I have a corner office with views of the entire city, that I drive an expensive vehicle and that I'm paid to travel.

My dates are always upset when I tell them I'm a bus driver.

Do you know what's remarkable?

Whiteboards.

What was the name of the Egyptian who was buried with chocolate and nuts?

Pharaoh Rocher.

Post Malone has delayed his tour.

Does this now make him Postpone Malone?

————————

How can you tell the difference between an alligator and a crocodile?

Easy: one will see you later, the other will see you in a while.

I was attacked by 1, 3, 5, 7 and 9.

The odds were against me.

What does a house wear?

Address.

I tried to get into a very trendy London nightclub last Saturday...

Doorman: "Sorry mate, you've had too many."

Me: "What, too many drinks?"

Doorman: "No, birthdays!"

What do you call a dinosaur that uses cheap toilet paper?

Mega-sore-ass.

My bank recently called me to let me know I had an outstanding balance.

I said: "Thanks! I used to do gymnastics," and hung up the phone.

That was nice of them to say.

I tripped in Paris.

Eiffel over.

I have an Irish friend with a great personality. He's so lively that he bounces off the walls.

His name is Rick O'Shea.

An Englishman, a Spanish man, a Frenchman and a German went to a club. The guy on stage asked if they could see him.

They said: "Yes. Oui. Sí. Ja."

_____

My wife just completed a 40-week body-building programme.

It's a girl and weighs 7lb 12oz.

The pulley is the most egotistical
of all machines.

It's always the centre of a tension.

———

My friend Ty came first in the Beijing
marathon, but he wasn't given the
gold medal.

The Chinese authorities refused
to recognize Ty Won.

My girlfriend asked me to name all my sexual partners, in order.

I should probably have stopped when I got to her name.

———————

My dad was born as a conjoined twin, but the doctors managed to separate them at birth.

I have an uncle, once removed.

My doctor said that I might die because
I accidentally consumed clay.

I'm shitting bricks, to be honest.

———

Relationships are a lot like algebra.

Have you ever looked at your X
and pondered Y?

What's heavier: a gallon of water or a gallon of butane?

Water, because butane is a lighter fuel.

What do you call a helpful lemon?

Lemon-aid.

I thought my dad spent all his savings on an expensive wig.

But I took one look and realized it was a small price toupee.

Driver: Officer, why are you crying while writing me a ticket?

Policeman: It's a . . . moving violation.

I have a perfect memory.

I can't remember a single time
I've ever forgotten anything.

_____

When my wife caught me standing
on the bathroom scales, sucking in my
stomach, she laughed. "Ha! That's not
going to help!"

"Sure it does," I said. "It's the only way
I can see the numbers."

Instead of a swear jar, I have a negativity jar. Every time I have pessimistic thoughts, I put a penny in . . .

It's currently half empty.

Did you hear the one about the giant throwing up?

It's all over town.

Did you hear about the guy who's left side was cut off?

He's all right now.

———————

Today I was in the bank when two men came in wearing masks . . .

Everyone felt hugely relieved when they told us it was only a bank robbery.

What do you call a magician who has lost their magic?

Ian.

What is "muffins" spelled backwards?

Exactly what you do when you take them out of the oven.

———————

My IT guy just asked: "How does a computer get drunk?"

It takes screenshots.

How many tickles does it take to make an octopus laugh?

Ten-tickles

How much does it cost to buy a large singing group?

Do you mean a choir?

OK, fine. How much does it cost to "acquire" a large singing group?

My son Luke loves that we named our children after *Star Wars* characters.

My daughter Chewbacca? Not so much.

———————

I was out with my young daughter and ran into a friend I hadn't seen in years.

"This is Beth," I said, introducing my kid.

"And what's Beth short for?" my friend asked.

"Because she's only three," I replied.

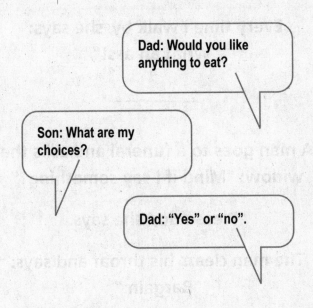

After all these years, my wife still thinks I'm sexy.

Every time I walk by, she says: "What an ass!"

––––––––––

A man goes to a funeral and asks the widow: "Mind if I say something?"

"Please do,' she says.

The man clears his throat and says: "Bargain."

"Thank you," the widow replies. "That means a great deal."

I said to my wife: "When I die,
I'd like to die having sex."

She replied: "Well, at least it'll be quick."

———————

Did you know I like dad
jokes about eyes?

The cornea, the better.

What do sprinters eat before a race?

Nothing. They fast.

_____

My wife blocked me on Facebook
because I post too many bird puns.

Well, toucan play at that game.

Guess who I bumped into on my way to get my glasses fixed?

Everybody.

What's the difference between mashed potatoes and pea soup?

Anyone can mash potatoes . . .

———————

Why did the lion cross the road?

To stop the zebra crossing.

I got a new job at the guillotine factory.

I'll beheading there shortly.

———

Did you hear about the yacht builder
who had to work from home?

His sails went through the roof.

I bought a second-hand time machine next Sunday.

They don't make them like they're going to anymore.

———————

My wife told me that she hates revolving doors and is afraid that she'll get stuck in them.

"Don't worry," I said. "You'll come around eventually."

Finland has just closed its borders.

No one will be crossing the Finnish line.

———————

What kind of tea do rich people buy?

Property.

Today I was invited by a female janitor to smoke some weed at her apartment, but I declined.

I can't deal with high maintenance women.

———————

A guy named Bart walked into a bar. He immediately got shot and died. Who killed him?

The Bartender.

If I had a penny for everyone who asked me to look after their dogs, I'd have a pound.

What do you call a pile of kittens?

A meowntain.

A policeman
stops a car . . .

Policeman: "Whose
car is this, where
are you taking it
and what do you
do for a living?"

Miner: Mine.

What language do oranges speak?

Mandarin.

What do pigs and ink have in common?

They both belong in a pen.

My wife claims that camouflage
is really sexy.

I just don't see it.

_____

I have a pure bread dog.

His name is Fi-dough.

What do you call a group of chubby newborns?

Heavy infantry.

Student loans, you got me through college.

I don't think I can ever repay you.

For Christmas,
I bought my wife
some new beads
for her abacus.

It's the little things
that count.

I got in touch with my inner self today.

That's the last time I use cheap
toilet paper.

My son just became a priest!

From now on he wants me to
call him "father".

What do you call a starving hippo in Budapest?

A hungry Hungary hippo.

What do you call it when your mother's sisters all gather at a funeral to avenge your death?

Vigil aunties.

I pinned a Rolex to the post just outside my house.

It's the neighbourhood watch.

When my father dies, he wants his ashes pressed into a record.

It was his vinyl request.

You know what makes me throw up?

A dartboard on a ceiling.

My ex-girlfriend just told me she
wants us to get back together again.
MAN! I sure am LUCKY!

I mean, first I win the lottery and
now THIS!

I misplaced Dwayne Johnson's cutting tool for the origami workshop . . .

I can't believe I lost the Rock's Paper Scissors.

You've heard of alphabet soup.
Now get ready for . . .

Times New Ramen!

_____

My wallet is like an onion.

When I open it, it makes me cry.

What was the most groundbreaking
invention of all time?

The shovel.

_____

Since everyone started washing
their hands . . .

. . . the peanuts in the pub have
really lost their flavour.

Did you know you can get
paid for sleeping?

It's a dream job.

I took a Viagra this morning,
but it got stuck in my throat.

I've had a stiff neck all day.

I hate telling people I'm a taxidermist, so when they ask what I do every day, I just say: "Y'know. Stuff."

———————

I went for an interview at a blacksmith's. The blacksmith said: "Are you any good at shoeing horses?"

"No," I said. "But I once told a donkey to piss off."

Did you hear about the dyslexic zombie?

He only eats Brians.

At a job interview recently, I filled up my glass of water until it overflowed a little.

"Nervous?" asked the interviewer.

"No," I said. "It's just that I always give 110 per cent."

———————————

Self-isolation is getting so bad I'm starting to get a crush on my roommate.

And we've been married for more than 20 years.

Yesterday I purchased a world map and put it on the wall in the kitchen. I gave my wife a dart and said: "Throw this and, wherever it lands, I'll take you there for a holiday."

Turns out we're spending three weeks behind the fridge.

———

A guy walks into his doctor's office and says: "Help me, doctor, I'm shrinking."

"Hold on," says the doctor. "Be a little patient."

Single man with toilet rolls would like to meet single woman with hand sanitizer for good clean fun.

What do you call a girl who sets fire to bank loans?

Bernadette.

Boss: Do you think you can come in on Saturday? I know you enjoy your weekends, but I need you here.

Me: Yeah, no problem. I'll probably be late, though. Public transport on weekends is slow.

Boss: What time will you get here?

Me: Monday.

As I put my car in reverse, I thought to myself . . .

"Ah, this takes me back."

We all know about Murphy's Law – anything that can go wrong will go wrong. But have you heard of Cole's Law?

It's thinly sliced cabbage.

———

John Travolta tested negative for coronavirus last night.

Turns out it was just Saturday Night Fever.

What do metals call their friends?

Their chromies.

_____

If you think Thursdays are depressing,
wait two days.

Then it will be a sadder day.

An invisible man married an invisible woman . . .

The kids weren't much to look at.

My wife says I'm the cheapest man in the world.

I'm not buying it.

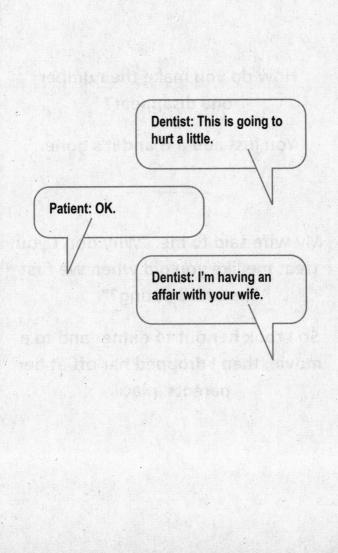

How do you make the number one disappear?

You just add a G and it's gone.

My wife said to me: "Why don't you treat me like you did when we first started dating?"

So I took her out to dinner and to a movie, then I dropped her off at her parents' place.

I ran out of toilet paper, so had to use old newspapers . . .

The *Times* are rough.

———

According to my therapist, I have real trouble verbalizing my emotions.

I can't say I'm surprised.

What's cooler than a talking dog?

A spelling bee!

_____

Earlier, I was driving behind an ambulance when a cooler fell off the back. I stopped and opened it up to find a foot inside.

So I called a toe-truck.

I've just seen a burglar kicking his own door down. I asked: "What are you doing?"

He said: "Working from home."

Roommate: If you keep stealing all my kitchen utensils, I'm moving out!

Me: That's a whisk I'm willing to take.

The nurse at the sperm bank asked me if I was ready to masturbate in the cup.

I said, "Well, I'm pretty good, but I don't think I'm ready to compete just yet."

———————

I've just accidentally sent a naked photo of myself to everyone in my address book.

Not only is it embarrassing, it's cost me a fortune in stamps!

Next summer I'm applying for
a job cleaning mirrors.

It's something I can really see myself
doing.

————————

You know, I was looking at our ceiling
the other day. It's not the best . . .

But it's up there.

**Did you hear about the girl
who hid drugs in her bra?**

People said it led to a bigger bust.

———————

**Did you know a school of piranhas
can devour a child in 30 seconds?**

**Anyway, today I lost my job at
the aquarium.**

What do you call a fake turd?

A shampoo.

_____

My girlfriend just couldn't accept my obsession with horoscopes.

In the end, it Taurus apart.

I'm developing a new fragrance for introverts. It's called:

"Leave me the fuh cologne."

––––––––––

What's the difference between a jeweller and a jailer?

One sells watches while the other watches cells.

What do you call a little boy who's half French and half Scottish?

A oui lad.

_____

Why couldn't the sailor play cards?

Because the captain was standing on the deck.

What's the difference between in-laws and outlaws?

Outlaws are wanted.

An elderly couple is in church. The wife says to the husband: "I've let out one of those silent farts. What should I do?"

The husband says: "Change the battery in your hearing aid."

―――――――

My wife just told me to put the toilet seat down.

I don't know why I was carrying it around in the first place.

I got fired from my job because
I kept asking my customers whether
they would prefer "smoking" or
"non-smoking".

Apparently, the correct terms are
"cremation" and "burial".

———————

Does anybody remember that joke
I told about my spine?

It was about a weak back.

I told my wife she should embrace
her mistakes . . .

She gave me a hug.

I got mugged by six dwarves last night.

Not happy.

What did Luke say to Han and Leia when they split up?

May divorce be with you.

———————

They told me I'd never be good at poetry because I'm dyslexic.

But to date I've made three jugs and a vase, and they're lovely.

Three weeks ago, I sent my hearing aid in for repairs.

I've heard nothing since.

I was walking past a farm and saw a sign that said: "Duck, eggs!"

I thought: "That's an unnecessary comma."

Then it hit me.

What do you call a group of men waiting for a haircut?

A barber-cue.

When single ladies get to the age of 50, they tend to get lots of cats.

This phenomenon is known as many paws.

A few minutes ago, I came to the conclusion that tofu is overrated.

It's just a curd to me.

A man walked into his home to realize that all his lamps had been stolen.

He was delighted.

―――――――

News just in: local police have acquired 1,000 bees.

They're being used in a sting operation.

We argued all day about what to call a medieval soldier.

But it was getting late, so we called it a knight.

I went the doctors the other day complaining about my sore feet.

He said: "Gout!"

I said: "But I've only just walked in!"

A priest, a minister and a rabbit walk into a blood bank.

The rabbit says: "I think I might be a type O."

Why did the terminator kill people even after retirement?

He was an ex-terminator.

_____

I've been teaching myself to juggle clocks.

People are saying I've got too much time on my hands.

I'm not wearing glasses anymore.

I've seen enough.

———————

My landlord says he needs to come and talk to me about how high my heating bill is.

"Of course," I told him. "My door is always open."

What do you call an angsty teenage robot?

A sigh Borg.

_____

What's the difference between bird flu and swine flu?

Bird flu requires tweetment; swine flu requires oinkment.

Waiter: Do you wanna box for your leftover food?

Dad: No thanks, but I'll wrestle you for it.

I've spent the past week learning escapology.

I need to get out more.

Did you hear about the cross-eyed teacher?

He couldn't control his pupils.

I like telling dad jokes even though I'm not a dad.

I'm a faux pa.

I can never remember the Roman numerals for 1, 1,000, 51, 6 and 500 . . .

IM LIVID

———

Not to brag, but I have sychic powers.

For example, right now you're thinking: "It's psychic, you idiot."

Who can drink two litres of gasoline?

Jerry can.

_____

What do you call a monkey that stepped on a minefield?

A ba-boom.

I just realized my countertop is made of marble.

I've been taking it for granite for years.

People are so sad I'm not entering the bake off this year.

Even their cakes are in tiers.

———————

My wife said to me: "If you won the lottery, would you still love me?"

"Of course I would," I said. "I'd miss you, but I'd still love you."

What do you call a group of mountains?

Hilarious.

Somebody just threw a jar of mayonnaise at me.

I was like: "What the Hellmann!"

All my friends think I'm weird for constantly eating ham and pineapple sandwiches.

But hey, that's Hawaii roll.

I asked 100 people which brand of shampoo they preferred.

All of them replied: "How the hell did you get in here?"

I was driving my date to her house and told her that I wasn't good with directions. She just laughed at me . . .

. . . so I right her left there.

How much space will Brexit free up in the European Union?

1 GB.

Why can't a nose be 12 inches?

Because then it would be a foot.

———————

We need to uninstall 2020 and then try reinstalling it.

The current version has a nasty virus.

Wife: I'm going to clone myself.

Me: That would be just like you.

I made a graph
of all my past
relationships.

It has an ex axis
and a why axis.

I didn't take my husband's name when I got married.

I thought it would be too confusing if we were both called Kevin.

_____

What's the difference between a crappy golfer and a crappy skydiver?

The crappy golfer goes: Wham! "Damn!"

The crappy skydiver goes: "Damn!" Wham!

If the Internet had a boat, where would they keep it?

In Google Docs.

_____

What do you call a poor part of a town in Italy?

The spa-ghetto.

What do you call it when two flowers have an unplanned pregnancy?

An oopsie-daisy.

Did you know that you can't breathe through your nose while you're smiling?

Ha! I made you smile.

———————

They said it was OK to go to the supermarket as long as we wore gloves and a mask.

They lied. Everyone else had clothes on.

I don't have a "dad bod".

I have a father figure.

_____

I was shocked the other day when
I thought I heard my girlfriend say
she wanted to go to see The Monkees
tribute band in Switzerland.

Then I saw her face – now I'm in
Geneva.

There's only one rule when
learning English.

Their our know rules.

_____

My sewing instructor just told me that
I'm the worst student she has ever seen.

Shit. Wrong thread.

What you do get from a dwarf cow?

Condensed milk.

_____

What do you call a sad berry?

A blueberry.

Having a mobile phone makes it really easy to cheat on my wife.

My son stands behind her and texts me to tell me what cards she has in her hand.

_____

What do you call it when you mix alcohol and American literature?

Tequila Mockingbird.

Every day
at breakfast,
I announce that
I'm going for a jog,
and then I don't.

It's my longest
running joke.

I asked my wife to describe me in five words. She said I'm mature, I'm moral, I'm pure, I'm polite and I'm perfect!

Then she added that I also have no idea how to use apostrophes and spaces.

———————

I've asked so many people what LGBTQ stands for.

So far no one has given me a straight answer.

My wife asked me: "Is it just me, or is the cat getting fat?"

Apparently, "No, it's just you," was not the right answer.

———————

The collective noun for a group of kangaroos is a "troop". What is the collective noun for a group of cars?

A lot.

I dig, you dig, he digs, she digs,
we dig, they dig.

It's not a long poem, but it's deep.

———————————

It's easy to convince ladies
not to eat Tide Pods.

But it's harder to deter gents.

I just watched a TV documentary about beavers.

Best dam show I ever saw.

So, I said to Arnie: "Where did you get those toilet rolls?"

He said: "Aisle B, back."

_____

My wife complained that my obsession with social media has destroyed the way we communicate as a family.

So I blocked her on my Facebook page.

Throughout 2019, I worked
on perfecting my eyesight.

It's finally 2020.

———————

I have OCD, so whenever someone
says "tho", I always respond with "ugh".

I saw a man with one arm shopping at a second-hand store.

I told him: "You're not going to find what you're looking for here."

———

You have three months to spend $500,000,000 and get nothing in return. How do you do it?

Run for President.

A woman is on trial
for stealing guitars.

The judge
asked her:
"First offender?"

She replied: "No.
First a Gibson,
then a Fender."

A man walks into a bar with a newt
on his shoulder . . .

Bartender: "What an interesting pet.
What's his name?"

Man: "Tiny."

Bartender: "What an odd name.
Why do you call him Tiny?"

Man: "Because . . . he's my newt."

———————

Some people say I'm too vague.

But you know how the saying goes . . .

@DadSaysJokes is a community-run dad jokes network on Instagram, Facebook and Twitter, with close to 3 million followers, inspired by the daily jokes of author Kit Chilvers' dad, Andrew.

Every day, followers submit their jokes and the team picks their favourites – or Dad just drops in his own zinger!

Kit, a young social networking influencer, started his career at the tender age of 14 when he created his original platform, Football.Newz. He has since added another nine platforms, including @PubityPets and monster meme page @Pubity, which has 23 million followers.

Also available: